MEXICO FOR KIDS
PEOPLE, PLACES AND CULTURES
Children Explore The World Books

SPEEDY
PUBLISHING

Speedy Publishing LLC
40 E. Main St. #1156
Newark, DE 19711
www.speedypublishing.com

The official name of
for Mexico is the United
Mexican States.

Mexico is
a federal
republic in
North America.
Mexico is the
fifth largest
country in the
Americas.

The Mexican people have varied origins and an identity that has evolved with the succession of conquests among Amerindian groups and later by Europeans.

The Basilica of Our Lady of Guadalupe is a Roman Catholic church visited by several million people every year, especially around 12 December, Our Lady of Guadalupe's Feast day.

Chichen Itza is one of the most visited archaeological sites in Mexico. Chichen Itza was one of the largest Maya cities and it was likely to have been one of the mythical great cities.

Pre-Columbian Mexico was home to many advanced Mesoamerican civilizations.

The earliest
human artifacts
in Mexico are
chips of stone
tools found
near campfire
remains in
the Valley of
Mexico and
radiocarbon-
dated to
circa 10,000
years ago.

Chichen Itza was a large pre-Columbian city built by the Maya people. Chichen Itza is located in the eastern portion of Yucatán state in Mexico.

Dominating Zócalo square, the massive Mexico City Metropolitan Cathedral is one of the oldest and largest churches in the western hemisphere.

For thousands
of years,
Mexico's
Indians such
as Aztecs and
Mayan were the
only people who
lived in Mexico.

A torero is a bullfighter and the main performer in the sport of bullfighting as practiced in Mexico and other countries.

Mariachi is a form of folk music from Mexico. Most songs are about machismo, love, betrayal, death, politics, revolutionary heroes and even animals.

The size of
a Mariachi
group varies
depending on
the availability
of musicians.

It is common
for people in
Mexico to make
and sell items in
open markets.

Weaving and embroidery are among the traditional crafts of Mexico's native Indian people.

Women bring brightly decorated clothes into the towns to sell in the markets.

Day of the Dead is a Mexican holiday celebrated throughout Mexico. A common symbol of the holiday is the skull.

Mexicans eat a variety of spicy foods that are often flavored with chilies. Many meals are served with tortillas.

Mexico is
the 11th most
populated
country in the
world with
around 117
million people.

Visit

BABY PROFESSOR
EDUCATION KIDS

www.BabyProfessorBooks.com

to download Free Baby Professor eBooks
and view our catalog of new and exciting
Children's Books

www.ingramcontent.com/pod-product-compliance
Lightning Source LLC
Chambersburg PA
CBHW060144120726
48003CB00009B/3018